THE GODDESS BOOK

A celebration of witches, queens,
healers, and crones

Nancy Blair

illustrations by Thalia Took

HAMPTON ROADS

ISBN 978-1-64297-020-3

Published in 2024 by Hampton Roads Publishing
Charlottesville, VA 22906
Distributed by Red Wheel/Weiser, LLC
www.redwheelweiser.com

Library of Congress Cataloging-in-Publication Data available upon request

Printed in China
MP
10 9 8 7 6 5 4 3 2 1

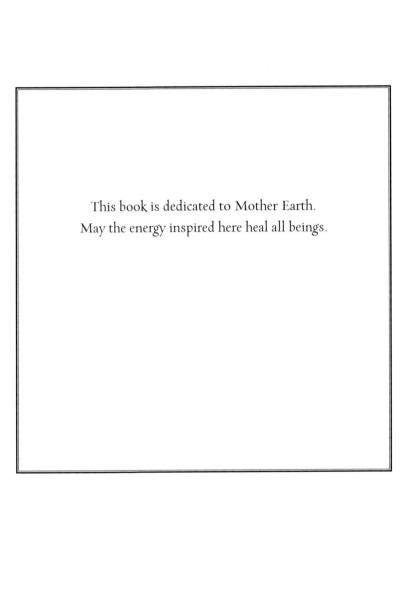

This book is dedicated to Mother Earth.
May the energy inspired here heal all beings.

CONTENTS

PREFACE

I am flying. Close to the ground, my feet stretched back and dangling behind me. I'm leaving the trailer park where I grew up. My body is fully alive, fully awake to the rush of wind in my hair. My left arm is snug against my waist, tight to my body the way a bird's legs pull up during flight. I look into my right hand and I'm gripping the edge of a plate, flat out and upside down in front of me. A dinner plate. My steering mechanism, my aileron, is a shiny white, porcelain plate. I tip the plate up to ascend and point it downward to bring me closer to the ground.

With my plate in my hand I leave the past behind. I don't look back, lest I crash into what lies ahead. I haven't a clue where I'm going. And for the first time in my life, I'm not worried about it.

In this dream of flying, I know how to take care of myself. Whenever I'm hungry, I point the plate down and land on Earth, my Mother Source. My legs are strong, my feet perfectly comfortable as they patter along the soft, thick blanket of green grass that sparkles with star-like dew. I eat what is juicy and good. Green and wild. Delicious and sweet. I squat beside a quiet river and cup my hands, bringing clear silver water to my lips. I feel completely alive, completely at peace.

I then hear a soft chanting song sifting from a stand of trees across the river. I wade in and out of the water, drawn by the hum of women's voices. I enter a grove and see a circle of women; smiling, singing, and dancing. They have been waiting for me. They turn and welcome me into the circle. I realize that each woman is a Goddess. I see Lilith and she nods a knowing welcome. There are Baba Yaga,

Gaia, Artemis, and the Willendorf. I greet each Goddess. I recognize each Goddess and she recognizes me.

Suddenly, I am fully awake in my dream, fully present in my woman body. I am one with the trees. I am one with the river and the invisible stars. One with every Goddess in the circle. I am filled with an overwhelming rush of love. Every cell pulsing with Divine Goddess love. I realize I am still carrying my plate, my directional. I hold it up for all the Goddesses to see. As I do, it takes on an energy all its own, floating away from me, finding its place in the night sky. My plate becomes the Full Moon. I realize I am not simply a visitor here. I am home. There's no place else to go. I turn my nose into the wind and join the chorus of Goddess voices in the chant that brought me across the river.

Roots Blossom Harvest Seeds.
Roots Blossom Harvest Seeds.

Preface

I am a dreamer. My creativity is informed by the musings of my daytime reverie, the jolting gallop of my nightmare rides, the shamanic visions of my menstrual cycle trances, and the haunting voices that leap from the depths of my fear, anger, doubt, and grief. The world of the invisible is the sacred wellspring from which my creative endeavors are born. Creativity is my path of prayer, my meditation, my communion with the Goddess. It is the most powerful source of healing in my life.

Our Goddess heritage and her story, the greatest story never told, brought me home. Awakening to Divine Female Presence flowing through me and around me, in my own personal "seasons" and bodily rhythms, in my everyday relationships and in my relationship with Earth, has brought me enormous peace. In Her many guises, faces, and names–from ancient art and artifact to poetic myth and mystery–I am comforted by Her nurturing compassion, wise-crack humor, and feisty, oftentimes cranky cautions. Goddess spirituality brought me home: to my Self, to the innate wisdom of my body, to our living Earth body, and the body of women's wisdom long repressed. The return of the Goddess is a rising tide that cannot be held back.

I am a dreamer and I am an artist, a toolmaker. The idea for this book brewed on the burner long before I wrote *Amulets of the Goddess: Oracle of Ancient Wisdom*. If necessity is the mother of invention, surely Dreaming Woman is necessity's sister. For it was both my own longing for a portable, Goddess-inspired meditation book and the prompting from my highly active and animated field of visions and dreams that finally brought *The Goddess Book* into focus. I dare to dream that it can touch as many women as possible. Like the shaman, the wounded healer, I offer the wisdom of

Goddess spirituality from a place of heartfelt compassion and gentle, instinctual knowing.

How we envision the goddess can be personal and subjective. The divine universal nature of the Goddess makes her Her reach global, and traditions from around the world inform Her mythology and how She manifests to each of us individually. The deeply sensitive and intuitive insight of Thalia Took makes her beautiful illustrations the perfect companion to this meditative, devotional guide.

I invite you to join with me in the seasonal circle of Goddesses. Listen to Her wisdom as you take your steps along the spiral path of Earth's forever-changing seasons. Let each meditation bless you, caress you, take you to the breadth of your own being from our vast spiritual heritage of woman's wisdom. It is said that when women waken, mountains move.

The seasons and cycles of Earth, Moon, and Sun are deeply rooted in the psychic patterns of our lives. As Earth carries us into Spring, Summer, Autumn, and Winter, we too become each season. Create meaningful, simple rituals that nourish your heart and soul. Create your life the way you want it.

Dare to dream. Let the Goddess inform your every step. I wish you many blessings on your sacred journey. May you find peace, healing, and wholeness in the delicious seasons of life in the wild forests, restless seas, wandering winds, fiery caverns, and fragrant gardens of the Goddess.

Spring

ROOTS

Snake along your dark rich path

Tiny root hairs nursing deep

Nestle in your Mother loam

Clear your voice

Prepare the ground

A seed is cracking

Something new is

Greening born

SPRING is a dynamically charged time of year that brings forth what has remained quietly invisible throughout the Winter months. What has remained unseen now breaks ground. Prepare a personal ritual or rite of passage to celebrate the mystery and power of the invisible made real. Your ritual can be a simple, solo ceremony or a community celebration involving others for added support and shared experiences.

Begin your ritual by expressing your intent. What is most important to you at this time? What do you want to bring into your life during the next few months? Light a green candle and use your journal to elaborate upon your intention. Invoke one of the Springtime Goddesses to help you stretch your imagination. Then cut images and words from magazines and catalogs and paste them in your journal. Use bright colors and words that enhance your desires. Create an exciting collage that expresses wants, needs, passions, and hungers with a sense that you have already accomplished them. Make your vision a pleasant and present experience. The more vivid an image you can create, the more effective it will be in your ritual-making magic. Let your images be a powerful and energizing visual prayer. Focus on your image daily throughout the next few months. Feel the excitement of what you can create in your life.

All change, all healing, begins as a thought, a change of consciousness. Translated into vivid images and life adjustments, dramatic results can take place. So be it.

TARA

The Mother Goddess

TARA is the Mother Goddess of Tibet and India. Cultures from India to Ireland derived the names of their beloved Earth Mother from Tara: Hebrew *Terah*, Latin *Terra Mater*, Etruscan *Turan*, and Ireland's *Tara*.

In Hinduism She is a Star Goddess, the unquenchable fire, calling new life into being. Often appearing as a celestial boat woman, She carries the suffering from the shores of ignorance and illusion to the shores of knowledge.

In Buddhism, Tara is the Mother of All Deities. She is devoutly prayed to for the relief of human suffering. Her many guises include a young and playful girl Tara–She Who Laughs and knows the lighthearted games of life.

◆ 43 ◆

Spring

waken the healing power of Tara's love. Springtime is filled with Her song. Light a candle and call Her name in your prayers. Ask for Her compassionate blessings. Take your girl Self into your lap, gently comforting her. What does she hunger and thirst for the most? Listen quietly to her wishes. Imagine that Tara surrounds you both with love. Let the strength of Her kindness heal the ancient wounds of your girlhood.

It is said that Tara was born from a tear. Let your tears flow. Let yourself float along the river of Her love, becoming One in an Ocean of Bliss.

AFFIRMATION

Tara speaks through me
with words of love and compassion.
I am always awakening.
I nurture the little girl who lives in my heart.
Every moment is a blessing.

PELE

Mountain Mother

IN HAWAIIAN legend, Pele is the Fiery Mountain Woman. From Her volcanic energy, new land masses are formed as old ones are swept away. The ocean islands are Her children. She is the Mountain Mother and the Devouring Crone. The Wise Woman places no value judgments on this Natural law. Pele teaches us how to live cooperatively with nature, adapting ourselves instead of foolishly resisting Her law.

◆ 17 ◆

Spring

Close your eyes and imagine that you are Pele. Stand in the yoga mountain pose, feeling grounded and strong. Feel the rhythmic inner pulse of a flowing, warm energy at your core. Allow the warm, red energy to flow up your spine, awakening and stimulating every cell in your body. Let it flow out the top of your head like a fountain. As it moves out around you, feel the red flow burning up any unwanted psychic debris. Now is the time for releasing anything that restrains your elemental female fire. Name what you are banishing. Say it out loud. Feel the space around you tingle and glow as you clear the land, reviving the life force. Open your eyes, feeling renewed and refreshed. Practice your Pele power throughout the week. At the center of the fire, something new is waiting to be revealed.

AFFIRMATION

I feel good about all of me.
I pay attention to those areas in my body and emotions
that are calling me.
I speak my truth and I'm comfortable with it,
even if it means going against outside authorities.

ANUKET

Nile River Goddess

THE NILE River Goddess of predynastic Egypt stands in an upraised gesture of joyful blessing, drawing down transformative energies of the Moon and bringing the annual floods that enriched the fields for spring planting.

The temples of the Goddess may be gone, but the magic in the Moon cannot be drained from your heart. We are all royal daughters. When we dare to create ourselves from what is truly real, choosing to become all of who we are meant to be, the sacred rivers will flow freely again, quenching our parched and thirsty souls.

Spring

Each morning this week, stand tall with your arms upraised in a gesture of Self-acceptance and certainty. Make choices that support all of who you are, my Sister Queen. You may have to stop playing "Nice Nice." You may have to disengage and walk away. But you need never suffer again. Make sure that what you support, supports you. If not, take steps to change it. Howl back. Release the chains that bind.

Spring is a perfect time to renew your strength from the underground sources of women's wisdom. The Nile River Goddess is calling you home. No matter where you are on the journey, every drop in the river eventually finds its way to the sea.

AFFIRMATION

Joy and peace of mind are within reach.
I take the necessary steps to create healthy change.
I focus and direct my energies on
what is truly important to me.

NAGINI

Serpent Goddess

A NAGINI is a lively and spirited Vedic Serpent Goddess. From Her waist up She is human. Her lower
torso is that of a snake. She lives in underwater temples
and palaces, below rivers and springs. She guards the sacred
treasures stored there. Her mission is threefold: to bestow
wisdom on those who are worthy, to prevent access to
sacred knowledge to those not deserving, and to prevent
sacred teachings from being lost.

◆ 25 ◆

Spring

Nagini, tell me what sacred knowledge lies hidden in the watery belly of the Earth? What treasures are hidden in your homeland tides? Won't you share your serpent mystery with me?

I am your daughter. I am snake woman-mermaid, like you. I shed my skin. I rattle and hiss. I dance inside the temples of the Goddess. I lick the morning dew from the river's green edge. And if anyone dare assault me, beware. My teeth are sharp and long. I can deliver a nasty bite.

I am Nagini.

AFFIRMATION

I defend my rights.
I enjoy practicing my Nagini skills.
I rejoice in my female power.

IX CHEL

Goddess of the Healing Arts

IX CHEL, Mayan Goddess of the healing arts, weaving, childbirth, and fate, embraces Her springtime consort the rabbit. Ix Chel is often pictured as a Serpent Crone, an upside-down vessel in Her hands, a wise woman dispensing healing visions. Sometimes She is shown seated peacefully at a loom, a bird perched in front of Her. Ix Chel is a triple shape-shifter, like many Goddesses.

Spring

Invoke Ix Chel's graceful, flowing movements for Springtime celebration and joyful collaborations. Imagine laughing, leaping, and dancing with your own animal ally–a familiar who can help you remember your instinctual, untameable inner nature. As you open to the subtle energies of an awakening Spring, release any burdens you may have carried through Winter's darkness. Let Spring's electric restlessness bring lightness to your step. Allow yourself to leap freely, letting obsessive or distracting thoughts melt away.

Imagine giving birth to a new you. Something new is yearning to germinate and flourish. Make a list of three things that you are going to create, or midwife into being, between now and Summer Solstice. Light candles and incense to Ix Chel for blessings. Enjoy the fruits of your labor.

AFFIRMATION

I am the designer, architect, and builder of my own future.
As the Earth opens in Springtime delight,
I open myself to new beginnings.
In the field of my own destiny,
my seeds are planted with loving care.

TIAMAT

Dragon Wisdom

BABYLONIAN myth said that before the world was created, there was only Tiamat, dragon of the bitter waters and sweet springs. In the deepest dark, before all being arose, She gave birth to light. Dividing Her body, She then became both Heaven and Earth, water and air, fire and roots.

The creative female dragon-power stirred enormous fear in the patriarchal church fathers. Their stories are full of dragon-slaying heroes. As daughters of the Dragon Moon, we can rewrite the story to reclaim our powerful heritage.

Spring

Here are some suggestions for a Dragon Woman in training: Dragons breathe fire. Ignite your inner spark. Speak up and let your words burn away lies, manipulation, and control.

Dragons are fearsome and refuse entrance to those who seek to destroy the forest magic. Resist unnatural acts that destroy Earth's resources.

Dragons exist outside of time. Therefore, keep your own pace, fulfilling your own desires. Retreat into your lair for renewal whenever you want.

Once awakened, a Dragon is your friend forever and will guard you with magical potions and spells. Therefore, use ritual, particularly just before and during your bleeding time. Invoke Tiamat for power and ride the Red River back Home. Give yourself a Dragon name and start roaring today. No one can take your power away from you--ever.

AFFIRMATION

I make life-enhancing decisions.
I face my fears with courage,
seeing them for what they are.
I am Dragon Wise.
I show my power.

BAUBO

Goddess of Bawdy Jokes

ER NAME, Baubo, means belly, as in belly laughter. She is the sacred clown Goddess of bawdy jokes.

Demeter refused all nourishment until her Daughter Persephone returned. Along came Baubo, wise old Crone Clown, chuckling, dancing, and lifting Her skirt, telling "wise cracks." The grieving Demeter cracked a smile that became a laugh. Soon the Great Mother was roaring Her own power. And with that, Persephone returned. Spring was reborn.

Spring

Baubo rekindles the female fires of the molten core, the deep Mother Mind. By lifting her skirt, She reminds Demeter of the Sacred Source of life. She reveals the paradoxical magic that exists in the combination of two unlikely elements. The word mourn means "to remember." Demeter's awakening reminds us that the source of life issues forth the relief of all sorrow.

Baubo parades Her belly wisdom as Spring breaks through the ground. She reminds us that sexuality–and laughter–are sacred. It is difficult for us to understand the healing power of bawdy jokes, since our culture uses them to debase us. However, it is pretty funny trying to imagine Baubo's sacred lips telling obscene jokes to the Goddess!

Let the Baubo dance. Listen to Her vulva-wise laughter. Can you imagine her juicy stories? Join her in a dance or two. Let your fire rise. It's the heat that cools.

AFFIRMATION

My laughter opens the door to healing and wholeness.
I do not participate in woman-hating humor.
My laughter reveals the sacred joy of being.

ASTARTE

Queen of Heaven

FOR thousands of years, the night sky was the realm of the Goddess. In Her sky and star aspects, She was known as Astarte, Isis, Ishtar, Nut, Hathor, Stella Maris, Venus, and Queen of Heaven. She gave birth to the entire Uni(yoni)verse from Her Heavenly Body. Her cosmic breath inspires all things with a rhythmic harmony. And at the end of time, She escorts the souls of the deceased back into Her galactic black cauldron for transformation and rebirth.

Spring

From beginning to end and back again, the Goddess Astarte and her family of cosmic interrelations govern living, being, and becoming. Astarte symbolizes the infinitely returning matrix of cosmic events. Her eternal weaving binds all life together. Astarte of the night sky guides our lives.

Astarte reminds you that the stars are your sparkling night Sisters. Each radiant crystal of starlight acts as a celestial navigator on your sacred path. Invoke Astarte's presence for evening rituals. As you gaze into the evening sky, find three stars and make your wishes. Make each wish a sacred blessing song. Speak your prayerful intentions aloud. Watch for visible manifestations of your supplications. What you request is easily available.

AFFIRMATION

In the Galaxy of the Goddess
I shine like the Moon, Sun, and Stars.
When there are no apparent answers
to the issues I face,
I trust Not Knowing.
I feel inwardly guided and outwardly protected.
Darkness always gives birth to Light.

ARTEMIS

The Moon Dancer

ARTEMIS is the courageous Goddess of the Virgin Dark Moon. She is the archer, who with unerring aim protects women and children, animals and their young. She guards the wilderness and honors the sacredness of all life. Her animals are the deer and bear. The Romans called Her Diana; She was also identified with Sophia, Goddess of Wisdom. When Her worship was banned by the Christian Church, women continued to flock to Her sacred groves.

Spring

Artemis dwells in the forests still. She whispers your name from the Moon-kissed leaves of the budding trees. She calls out to you from the sky. She stirs passion and longing for the childlike, untamed, instinctive, and free. The Earth Mother is awakening in Springtime splendor. What is awakening in you?

Make an offering to Artemis this week. Ask for Her wise guidance with any unresolved issues from your childhood. If you are having difficulty forgiving others, begin by forgiving yourself. Feel comforted in the presence of your Moon Sister. Imagine that you meet by candlelight in the sacred grove. Her unconditional, loving hug welcomes you home. Tickle each other silly.

Make a sacred pact with Artemis. Begin with: I will forever remember.

AFFIRMATION

I am wild.
I am wise.
I talk to myself in loving, encouraging ways.
I give my full attention to whatever I am doing.
I make my own self-generating choices.
I am safe and secure
in the ever-changing flow of life.

APHRODITE

Goddess of Love

APHRODITE is the Goddess of love, sacred sexual pleasure, and destiny. She was honored throughout the ancient world as Queen of the Sea and Guardian of Natural Law, which cannot be altered by human interpretation.

The month of April is dedicated to Her. Her animal ally is the dove. The Semitic word for dove, *ione*, is a cognate of the word yoni or vulva.

Spring

At Aphrodisias, in Turkey, there is a temple dedicated to Aphrodite. Pomegranate, fig, and olive trees grace the landscape. While visiting there, I imagined Aphrodite seated on her throne, administering justice with clear-sighted compassion. She listened respectfully to all the details, watching gestures and facial expressions for subtle and shadowed truths. With eloquent calm, Aphrodite called harmony back into being. I felt Her peaceful presence in the warm wind that stirred the air and pressed against my cheek like a mother's sweet kiss.

Call Aphrodite's name. Let Her beauty flow through you. Let Her divine essence stir the sea of memory within you. State your innermost yearnings aloud, your voice distinct and clear. Whatever disputes you may be having in your relationships will soon pass. Dwell silently in this peaceful moment.

AFFIRMATION

I stand in awe of the beauty all around me.
I honor and share my talents and skills.
I appreciate my strength and wisdom.
I am blessed in Goddess Grace.

VILA

Forest Fairies

THE VILA are Eastern European forest Fairies. They speak the language of the plants and animals and are skilled in the healing arts. They often appear as horses, whirlwinds, snakes, or swans. A Vila is usually born in the Spring, when the rains are misty soft, the morning grass twinkling with dew. When you see a rainbow, that means a Vila was born. A Vila also sees that sufficient rainfall occurs to bring about new plant life.

Spring

Fiercely protective of the forest creatures, a Vila will lure an offender into the deep woods. There She will bring him into the magic circle and nearly dance him to death in repentance for injuring one of her family members.

Women who want to learn from the forest craft of the Vila are required to form a sisterhood pact by going to the woods at sunrise on the day of the Full Moon. There the aspiring Vila is to draw a circle in the earth with a birch or a broom. Then call out to the Vila and listen for Her reply. Once accepted into the circle of forest Fairies, a Vila will grant any wish. What is your wish?

AFFIRMATION

My most important teachers reside in Nature.
The unity of all living energies is visible in a single raindrop.
I live in harmony with Nature's call.

TRIPLE GODDESS

Maiden, Mother, Crone

THE TRINITY of the Goddess represents the three most powerful passages of a woman's life, venerated as "blood mysteries" from ancient matriarchal cultures.

The Trinity of the Goddess is the Great Round: She who embraces All, affirming that women create.

The Maiden lives in her imagination and dreams, unto herself, for no one else. She is unlimited potential. The Maiden is sometimes called the Virgin, which originally meant unwed, not celibate. A girl's first menarche signals her cosmic connection to the cyclic rhythms of the Moon.

In her sacred Mother power, she creates the world. Whether through children of the physical body or the "children" of creative ideas, the Mother brings forth from her body-mind those gifts and talents uniquely her own.

The Crone, whose wise blood remains within, has great dignity and power as healer, eider, aunt, grandmother, and shaman. Her wisdom weaves the mystery of death and rebirth back into life.

Experiencing the Triple Goddess is not a linear project. All three aspects are present from the moment you are born. From the mouths of babes comes the wisdom of the ages. Mothers call up instant wisdom when emergencies arise. And wise old women may feel as free as girls.

Climb into the threefold lap of the Goddess for eternal renewal. Create a simple menstrual ritual to honor the Triple Goddess in you.

AFFIRMATION

I am the mystery of Maiden, Mother, Crone.
I am proud of my cosmic woman cycles.
I am free of beliefs that limit my experience.
I am restored to complete health in the free-flowing
cycle of life.

DANU

The Great Goddess

DANU IS the Great Mother Goddess, from whom all Irish gods descend. She is one of the most ancient of Goddesses, and much about her remains a mytery. She is a source of nobility, unity, and power, and also the namesake of the Tuatha Dé Danann, "the folk of the goddess Danu," considered to be the most ancient of Celtic spirits. She is a giver of gifts, and bestows creativity, craft, and skill. As a Mother Goddess, Danu is believed to have suckled all other gods and instilled in them great wisdom. All blessings come from Danu. She offers you the gifts of confidence, courage, and the overview of the big plan as well as a deeper look into the often tossed-aside details.

Spring

Her visit today reminds you of your own wondrous ability to create the World around you the way you want it. Relax and enjoy the view. You are ready to take on the expansive nature of your Ancient Mother Goddess self. You can take hold of the reins of leadership with assurance that your focus and vision are clear-sighted and balanced. It's a good time to step forward and give a strong voice to your ideas. You needn't prove yourself to anyone for any reason. It will all work out if you let it. As you radiate trust and loving warmth to those around you, you'll notice your effect on people. Your Danu nature will surely catch on. Someone may confide in you a long-held secret. Be generous with hugs. Advice is not the Goddess way. You empower others by reminding them of their own strength and wisdom. Ask instead, "Is there anything I can do to help?"

AFFIRMATION

I am a courageous leader.
I trust myself.
I allow magic to unfold in everything I say and do.
I enjoy the company of my own loving smile.

Summer

BLOSSOM

Snake along your dark rich path

Tiny root hairs nursing deep

Nestle in your Mother loam

Clear your voice

Prepare the ground

A seed is cracking

Something new is

Greening born

IN SUMMER, joy and blessings abound. Everything in Nature is growing, flowing, and blossoming. Fruits are sweet, fat, and deliciously juicy. The vegetable gardens are ripe for picking. And vacation comes not a day too soon.

Summer is the season of the longest day, yet the longest day also begins the decline of the Sun's power, essentially heralding the onset of Autumn at the same time. A cosmic paradox always delights the Great Mother!

With paradox in play, you may experience unusual light, hearty, and comic episodes during the next few months. Be prepared to let go and hold on at the same time. You may find yourself facing an old issue with new insight. Schedule plenty of leisure time between the feisty fits of personal growth spurts. For those inclined toward shyness, Summer may be challenging. Remember: Blossoming is your birth-right.

Invoke Yemaya during your Summer Solstice ritual. Prepare an altar in Her honor. Bring flowers, shells, stones, and crystals–whatever She calls for. Fill one of your favorite bowls with salt water and place it at the center of the altar. Place photos of women in your family–including friends that are "family"–around the bowl of water. Include one of yourself. Introduce Yemaya to your family circle. In prayerful supplication, ask Yemaya to heal the lives of those you love. Ask Her to release old fears and burdens, bringing freedom, joy, and peace to the women at the altar and the women of the world. Close your ritual with a song of gratitude.

ISIS

The Source of All Life

IN ANCIENT Egypt, the Goddess Isis was known as the Source of all life. Although she was called by a thousand names, one of Her most sacred names was *Iusaaset*–Utterer of Words, Conceiver of Worlds. She gave birth to the Sun-god, Horus. She brought the arts, language, medicine, weaving, architecture–all culture to Her people.

Summer

As you welcome Isis into your life this week, spread your arms wide in a gesture of awakening and receptivity. Breathe Her grace deep into your body. Isis encourages you to honor the past by integrating what you have learned and can use from it. Release the rest. As the light of the Summer sun dances new green shoots through the Spring Earth, break free from lingering doubt and fear. Say out loud what is bothering you.

This may be a perfect time for limiting your dependence on material things and other people. Leaning on externals can set you off-balance. An Isis woman is self-supporting. Stand tall. You needn't ask permission to be who you are. You are the author of your own life. Say it the way you see it. Make it the way you want it. Isis is smiling with you.

AFFIRMATION

I am valuable and worthy of love.
I am filled with enthusiasm and renewed vitality.
I can breathe deeply and trust my own inner knowing.
The perfect answers are revealed to me
as I listen to the voices of wisdom within.
I can speak and create my world.

YEMAYA

Goddess of the Sea

WHEN the peoples of Africa were enslaved and brought to the Caribbean Islands and the Americas, they held on to their love of Yemaya, Goddess of the Sea, Womb of Creation. She kept their spirits alive in the horrible conditions of slavery. In traditional Yoruba culture and spirituality, Yemaya is a mother spirit: matron spirit of women, especially pregnant women. The vastness of her motherhood, her fecundity, and her reign over all living things is celebrated in celebration, ritual, and song.

Summer

As Queen of the Sea, Yemaya governs the Moon, childbirth, and all female cycles; coming, going, and resting in between. She is the Goddess of Forever Be-Coming.

One of Yemaya's most powerful attributes is to be able to see into secrets and dreams. Ask Her to release you from old beliefs, thoughts, or feelings that seem to enslave you and keep you estranged from the center of your sacred Self. You may want to tell Her a story about your life, a story of healing and hope that arose from despair.

The tears of sorrow and joy flow from the same tide. Water has the power to smooth the sharpest stone, flood the driest plain. Let the healing waters of this most beloved Goddess take you to the Sun- and Moon-drenched shores of forever becoming free.

AFFIRMATION

I revel in the beauty of my always changing life.
I nurture what I value most.
I am free to make my own choices.
I say No to some things in order to say Yes to others.
I deserve to live joyfully free.
I deserve to feel good about myself.

SELENA

Full Moon Goddess

S ELENA, the Full Moon Goddess, is the messenger
of good tidings. Wearing a crescent crown, she rides
the Night sky in Her silver chariot drawn by horned cows.
Legend tells us that Her moonlight reflects all that is true
and eternal.

Selena's journey across the heavens determines the
surging and synchronous pulse of the blood cycle all women
share.

Summer

Selena encourages us to become aware of the subtle, and sometimes not so subtle, ebb and flowing currents occurring in our own bodies. She teaches us to ride the magical rhythms and unbidden psychic gifts of our bodily functions with instinctual awareness, trusting our tidal flows. Listen to your delightful lunacy. What are you yearning for most? Say a prayer facing Her radiant fullness and listen for Her guiding enchantments throughout the week.

Full Moon mania is a time for manifesting dreams, visions, and fantasies. Whether we create "children" from our physical bodies or from our imaginative mind-bodies, it is time to give birth to and nurture that little something you've been thinking about all along. Now is the perfect time for shouting out loud what you've only dared whisper. Selena invites you to leap into the chariot with Her to broadcast your innermost hankerings. Hold on to your horned crown!

AFFIRMATION

I express outwardly my creative impulses.
I choose to "shine" my energies wisely,
knowing that my energy is a sacred gift.
I am blessed in Full Moon radiance.
My life is fun!

SEKMET

Egyptian Sun Goddess

SEKMET is the Lioness of the Sun, Lady of the Flame, ferocious Measurer of Time. She governs the fate of humankind–a guardian of the gateway of rebirth.

As the hearty She-Cat moves into the night cave, She asks us to savor the breadth of each day, releasing and recycling what isn't useful.

◆ 84 ◆

Summer

Sekmet walks with dignity and grace. Her body is supple and strong. She seeks nourishment from what Her senses desire and enjoys luscious moments alone. Keenly attuned to what lies hidden beneath the surface, She sniffs out danger, lies, and suppressed truths. Her Fiery Female power of Self-preservation is a force as strong and untouchable as lightning. She is outrageously courageous.

Sekmet encourages us to live each day with inner dignity, following a sacred path of personal integrity. Let radical thoughts (ideas grounded in personal truth) animate healthy behavior. A Sekmet woman is ferociously loving and daringly honest. She reminds us that our own best friend speaks from the lioness heart within. Listen to what you are afraid to say. Let your heart speak its fiery passions. Let Sekmet of the Sun melt the ice on frozen feelings. Roar your wild desires. Creative action is called for.

AFFIRMATION

Each day belongs to me.
I am open to the exciting possibilities
that each moment brings as I live my truth.
I prance through this day with strength and ease.
I address issues that disturb me.
My truth gives me freedom.

OSHUN

Yoruba River Goddess

JOY and sensual pleasure are the gifts of Oshun, Yoruba River Goddess, Mother of the Deities. She sits upon a moss-covered rock by the river, often depicted holding a mirror in one hand and a golden fan in the other. All of Earth's dazzling jewels are woven through Her hair. Just as the rivers flow to the sea, Oshun will take you to a place of deep inner peace as She reminds you of the powers of pleasure.

Summer

Oshun teaches us to live in the flow of the present moment. Let your body-mind pace your course, awakening to the surge, ebb, and flow of your hormones, dreams, and desires. If you've been putting your body at risk for the sake of external achievement and approval, slow down. Listen to the subtle underground currents that nourish your woman's well. Make peace with your body and revel in erotic pleasures with this most sensual Goddess.

Practice thinking and moving like a river. Throughout the day, give yourself time to let your thoughts float, without grasping on to any one thought in particular. If, before going to bed, one thought or idea keeps returning, make a note of it. Ask Oshun to bring it back to you in a way that can bring joy and comfort into your life.

AFFIRMATION

I stay with good feelings.
I explore new areas that excite me.
I do what is easy, loving, fun, and true.
I enjoy the pleasures of my body.

NUT

Egyptian Sky Queen

WELCOME NUT, Egyptian Goddess of the turquoise sky of the day and the royal blue sky of night. Nut arches over the Earth, animating all things with Her cosmic regenerative energy. In Egypt, heaven was the body of a woman.

Summer

Before getting out of bed in the morning, take a few moments to start your day the Sky Queen Way. Imagine lying on the soft green ground, gazing into an endless azure sky. You feel the brilliant warmth of summer softening the tension in your muscles. You feel safe and peaceful.

You stretch your body fully. Your hands join Nut's fingers. Your feet touch Her toes. You feel dynamically charged with life-force energy. While breathing deeply, let a single word or short phrase come to you. For example: "Quiet." "Room to grow." "Good enough." "No more lies." "Laughter." You may hear the Goddess Nut whisper an important message in your ear. Let each word or phrase be your mantra for the day.

When it feels right for you, gently "unplug" yourself. When you open your eyes, you feel strongly expansive and energized. You are ready to let the Sky Queen bring you to a fresh new day. Something wonderful is about to happen!

AFFIRMATION

I stretch my imagination and soar with new ideas.
I have many choices for change.
I review the map of my personal path.
I look forward with enthusiasm
to the adventures that await me.

FORTUNA

Goddess of Bounty

I N ROMAN TIMES, Fortuna was the force behind all
propitious events. She used Her special magic to create
abundance wherever She smiled. Her powers of fertility and
increase were called upon in all human affairs.

If you're looking outside yourself for prizes and rewards
to confirm your personal sense of security, Fortuna reminds
you that it is time to review your values. Prosperity resides
in your consciousness. The wisdom of the Goddess lifeway
teaches us to look within.

Summer

Driven by scarcity and greed, never having, doing, or being enough, we are driving ourselves to the brink of personal and planetary destruction. Simplify your life. Eliminate excesses. Do you have feelings of scarcity and deprivation that trigger the need for more, more, more? Fortuna teaches us to transform a fear-based poverty mentality into a "plenty enough" state of being.

As a Priestess of Fortuna, you are required to make friends with money. This is a good time to sort the "apples from the oranges." Balance your checking account. Open a savings account for the future. Make conscious decisions about what and whom your money supports. Take a course in money management to better perform your money magic rituals. Fortuna reminds you that it takes only a short glance (and a little financial savvy) to see that the word *nowhere* is *now here*.

AFFIRMATION

I am enough.
I do enough.
I have enough.
I am blessed with many gifts and I am grateful.
I easily take care of my finances.
I am healthy, wealthy, and wise in all ways.
I attract supportive, loving relationships
and joyful situations.

GAIA

Earth Mother

S HE HAS been called by a thousand names: Gaia,
Mother of All, Mother Nature, Big Mama Blue. She
is the Blessed Earth Mother who sustains our lives with
Her own. She existed before time began. Time was one of
Her children!

Now scientists have called on Gaia again: She gives Her
name to the Gaia Hypothesis, the theory that all the Earth
is one living creature.

◆ *97* ◆

Summer

Throughout the ages, the many diverse Earth-honoring peoples held festivities to express gratitude for the gifts Gaia has given. Placing honey cakes and grains at doorways and crossroads, in gardens and fields. Strewing herbs in houses and temples. Lighting candles, singing, dancing, and making merry are all an integral part of the vibrant religions of our ancestors who worshipped her. Every act of living and being reflected a deep and direct understanding of Gaia as sacred Source and Re-Source. For as many as 200,000 years, our ancestors tended the Garden of Earthly Delights with joy, reverence, and meaningful rituals.

Take a long, slow breath. Never for a moment are you alone. The air you breathe is a gift from Her body. Resonate with Her unconditional blessings. This week make a simple offering to Earth. Begin with "I promise . . ."

AFFIRMATION

I am a child of Gaia.
She holds me.
She will never let me go.
I belong.
I am in awe of Her Divine Design
flowing all around me and through me.
I think twice about my actions,
including Earth in all my decision-making.

AMATERASU

Sun Goddess

TO THE JAPANESE Shinto, Amaterasu is the Sun Goddess, "Heaven Shining Great August Deity." Her troublesome brother, Susanowo, the Thunder God, was jealous of Her power. When he killed a precious colt and several women in the celestial weaving house, Amaterasu drew Herself back into the Rock Cave of Heaven. A heavy darkness fell upon the land. Nothing grew. Nothing lived.

Summer

Hoping to bring her back, Uzume, Heavenly Alarming Female, lewdly danced before the cave entrance. The laughter of the eight hundred deities around Uzume shook the heavens. In curiosity and wonder, Amaterasu emerged to find a mirror before Her. Astonished by Her own brilliance, She stepped further from the cave. The door behind Her closed, and all life was illuminated once again.

Praise your sunny side! Both the adventures of the Sun and the mysteries of the Moon belong to you. They are not opposites. As we reclaim our Solar selves, we must no longer abide by a language of dualistic "archetypes." Boldness, guts, and confidence are not the cosmically ordained property of the male. The world of dreams and intuition is not only female. Women bleed by the Moon. Our possibilities are as limitless as the Sun. As you take back the night, bring the Sun with it.

AFFIRMATION

I am the Sun and I am the Moon.
I release dualistic thinking that confines my potential.
I can be anything I want to be.

MELISSA

Blessed Bee Goddess

IN ANCIENT matristic cultures, the Bee was considered the Priestess of the Goddess Aphrodite. Known as Melissa, Mel Ionia, or Deborah, the Bee used Her sacred fertilizing power to bring new life into Being year after year. In the Garden of the Goddess, the Queen Bee is a reminder of the Eternal Return. She weaves the thread of regeneration with each Delicious Kiss. Her honey, an important preservative, was the elixir and ambrosia of renewal—the nectar of wisdom and magic. Her honeycomb, an elaborately constructed architecture of perfectly arranged hexagrams, reflects the intricate balance of all things in Nature.

Summer

The buzzing of the Bee was known as the voice of the Goddess, the sound of creation in action. Her "words" are a powerful Source of inspiration and caution. For those who honor the laws of Nature there waits a sweet reward. Avoid snares and stings by listening to your inner voice, your intuitive direction.

Let Her potent presence entertain you as She whispers words of love and laughter in your ear. Become keenly aware of what your senses tell you. Let every whiff and sniff of your surroundings be a meditation. Follow the Queen Bee's dance in the direction of blissful delight. She reminds you to enjoy the pleasures of your pursuits. So be it.

AFFIRMATION

I achieve my goals easily and quickly.
I trust instinctive response.
I face challenges with confidence.
I enjoy the sweetness of my life.

MOTHER GODDESS

The Cosmic Flow-er

IN MANY ancient myths, the Mother Goddess created the first peoples from clay and brought them to life with Her Moon Blood. We are all born as Cosmic flow-ers, daughters of the Goddess. And it is to our magical, Earth-bound bodies we must turn for wisdom.

Both conventional and new-age medicine seem to consider the body an enemy to be conquered by experts wielding vitamins, medicines, or scalpels. Illness is seen as evidence of sin–with proper care, you would never be sick, grow old, or die. These conventional ideas are unrealistic and destructive, for everything everywhere is growing, breeding, dying, or decaying.

Summer

Follow the Spiral Way of the Cosmic Flow-er. Let your body inform your healing choices. Engage your menstrual mind. You are the roots, stem, blossoms, and seeds. The Garden of the Goddess is a wild forest where nothing is neat and weeds heal. In the Wise Woman tradition, pain is inevitable, suffering optional.

Each time you face life's pains and losses is an opportunity to lose control and find the Goddess's unpredictable wisdom. Illness is acceptable. Ignoring it is not.

Learn how to nourish yourself, transforming pain with love. Each time you honor your body's wisdom, your body responds with relief. Never empty, forever changing, you awaken to the gifts of endings, and you move on. A new season begins again.

AFFIRMATION

I am a Cosmic Flow-er.
My body is my ally.
I nourish myself every step of the way
I take time to find out what I need.

Summer

DIANA OF EPHESUS

She Who Brings Forth Life

THE ROMANS called the Goddess of the Moon Diana. The Greeks worshipped Her as Artemis. Throughout the Mediterranean, the Goddess of plants and wild animals was She Who Brings Forth Life. The awesome sculpture of the "many-breasted" Artemis is from Ephesus. Her body, the Tree of Life, is teeming with the fruits of Earth's bounty.

Summer

We have passed through the gate into Summer. The Earth has begun shifting away from the Sun, but the light is still strong. There is time to grow. Invoke Diana when wrestling with self-doubt, especially when you hear the inner critic saying that you don't do enough or have enough. Banish the judge by beginning each day with the Mantra: I AM ENOUGH. Take the solid strong stance of Artemis when doing so.

The seedbed of your power lies in your ability to remain indifferent to how others "name" you. The Goddess offers you the power of self-naming, self-nurturing. Bask in the liquid strength of loving self-talk. Bless yourself. Refrain from criticizing yourself. Who needs it? Leap into the garden of the Goddess and feast on the abundance there. Keep company with the wise. Is it time for a massage, a candlelit bath, a feast with friends? Dare to taste the truth.

AFFIRMATION

Life gives me enriching experiences in which to grow.
I stop comparing myself to others.
I stop blaming myself.
I nourish my whole being with goodness.
My blessings are many.

GENTLE FAWN SPIRIT

Goddess of the Summer Winds

THE IROQUOIS call the Goddess of the South Wind Neoga or Fawn, in Korea she is known as Yongdeong, the Aztecs knew her as Vitztlampaehecatl. Around the world, She presides over the Summer Winds, walking closely with the Sun. She is kind and gentle and moves forward with strong resolve, like the early light of dawn.

Gentle Fawn reminds you that activity and motion without direction are ineffective. Conscious decision-making is empowering. A routine task done with the mindful intent of fostering self-care brings a whole new level of meaning.

Summer

Y ou may not be able to make big leaps right away, but the little steps build on each other. Powerful possibilities are all yours. Buying a comfortable pair of shoes that better fits your Wise Woman lifestyle can take on the quality of a ceremony.

Doing what counts does not come from logic and reason alone. What matters most involves intuitive spark and inner commitment. There is no way to make everyone happy, so stop trying. Insight precipitates change but is not itself change. You'll discover that change–real change–requires determination and a different approach. Stay faithful to your spiritual path. Write out reminders for yourself and post them everywhere. Choice is yours, simply and powerfully. Meditation is essential. Stop for a moment and give thanks for something special in your life. What is valuable sometimes comes at a slow and steady pace.

The Goddess Book

AFFIRMATION

*Every day my journey begins
with new perspective and power.
I am willing to address my behavior
to create long-lasting change.
Integrity is my path of power.*

Autumn

HARVEST

Bring it in

Bring it home

Crunchy cackling ghostly shadows

Sort the seeds and berries

Gather what the witches love

Leave a little by the bush

To feed the Forest Fairies

THE AUTUMN Equinox heralds the "Season of the Witch." This is a time when the life-force energy is returning to the roots in preparation for the deliciously inner recesses of Winter. In our human lives, Autumn signals a time to clarify and integrate what we gathered from our Summer experiences, determining what is valuable, wise, wondrous, and useful, as well as learning to let go of what is not.

Using your journal, explore what's going on in your life at this time, judging and acting on your own behalf–your own *be-wholing*–what is best for you!

The following is a good, simple recipe-ritual for letting go: Gather lengths of natural fiber rope, thick and thin, long and short, each one corresponding to a particular issue that you are addressing and releasing. Be specific. Do not use a person's name, but name what it is that binds you to that person, speaking strongly and assuredly aloud. Then, one by one, with a pair of scissors, cut each length into smaller and smaller pieces until you can't recognize it as rope.

As you cut, say what it is you are releasing or disconnecting from. For example: "My past holds no power over me. I disconnect easily from the haunting and hurt. I no longer need to linger on it." When you are finished, bury the cut-up pieces along with your favorite flower bulbs–tulips, daffodils, hyacinths, etc. If you live in an apartment, find a wooded place or an empty lot. Wait to see what blossoms anew in the Spring.

WILLENDORF GODDESS

Primordial Ancestress

THE WILLENDORF Earth Goddess is the oldest sculpture of a human form yet uncovered. She represents the primordial Ancestress who gave birth to all of Creation out of Her bountiful body.

Our love story with Earth begins by addressing our relationship with our own woman body in all its fleshy softness. When you love your body, you are able to listen to its real needs.

◆ 125 ◆

Autumn

Self-loathing that stems from body shame causes many women to withdraw from the joy of living and being, avoiding relationships, sexual pleasure, and physicality.

The Goddess loves all bodies. Begin welcoming the Goddess into your body-mind with the following meditation. Imagine having a conversation with a part of your body that you have consistently disliked. Begin with a few simple questions: "How can we be friends?" "How can I show my love?" Keep a journal of your experiences. Practice simple ceremonies of self love. Your body is the most important teacher you'll ever know.

The "miracles" we seek from external sources are nothing compared to the miracles waiting to happen when we develop a joyous relationship with the Goddess within. When we act in loving ways to diminish the suffering in our body, we contribute to the healing of Earth.

AFFIRMATION

I love the Earth, my Mother,
as I love my Woman Body.
I am uniquely beautiful inside,
outside, and all over.
I will not live by standards that are not my own.
My body is a miracle.

KUAN YIN

Goddess of Compassion

K UAN YIN, the Goddess of compassion, is the most revered deity in the Chinese pantheon. *Kuan* means Earth and *Yin* is the dynamic female life force. Kuan Yin's strength, like silk, is disguised in softness. She is often shown riding a dolphin, a unique vision of the wild strength of women. She who rides–yet doesn't control–the untamable forces of life holds the key to happiness.

Autumn

Kuan Yin's gift of tranquility is the secret that is no secret: the potential for deep understanding, compassionate wisdom, and courageous, empowered action are present within us at all times. Each of us is born from wholeness–conception and completion at the center of the seed. Accepting and honoring all of who we are is Kuan Yin's healing power of compassion at play.

During the next few days call on Kuan Yin. Take a few moments to practice compassionate, healing prayer. Imagine unconditional love streaming from Her, entering your body at your navel. Feel it travel through you. When you've taken all you need, direct the energy out the top of your head. Send healing love to whomever or wherever you want. During the week, make offerings of gratitude for Kuan Yin's blessings of loving peace.

The Goddess Book

AFFIRMATION

Divine love lives within me.
I am comforted by the miraculous beauty of my own being.
I create supportive environments that foster
self-expression and affirm my value.
I easily give and receive love.

SNAKE GODDESS

Change, Creation, Renewal

THE SNAKE Goddess is an emissary and avatar of the vital shamanic energy that She channels from the spirit world. The snake is a sacred symbol of the creative impulse of the Great Goddess. Snakes shed their skin and emerge renewed, much as women shed our monthly skin, bleed without dying.

The Snake Goddess teaches Self-affirmation. She encourages you to find meaningful purpose rooted in spiritual nourishment.

Autumn

Stay wise-eyed and mindful as you go about your day. Give form to the natural impulses that spring from your imagination. Speak prophetically, saying what lands on the tip of your tongue, rather than swallowing your truth. A woman in her Snake Power fearlessly expresses her wants and needs without hesitation. However, her pathway to discovering them is meandering and without anxiety. Allow time in your schedule for dreaming, inspiring, and gathering information from your inner, visionary landscape.

Change old habits, releasing guilt and shame. You are a Priestess of the Goddess, a vessel of transformation, an equal partner and participant in the sacred order of the cosmos. Now is the time for conjuring magic. Cast a spell, directing your willpower for healthy, life-affirming change. Our Serpent Sister encourages you to say yes. Or rather: Yesssssssss.

AFFIRMATION

In flesh and blood I am the Goddess.
I dream for my blessed future
by living joyfully in the present.
I am confident.
I am surrounded by peace.

SHEKINAH

The Force of Change

IN HEBREW tradition, Shekinah is the female force of Divinity. She is the clear sharp breeze on a cool autumn noon. She is the winter song on the wings of the snowbirds heading South. She floats a round belly cloud in Her invisible blue river sky. She is the hissing rattle of autumn's copper leaves against a concrete wall. She lifts the dust and debris into tiny tornados and settles them far from home. Shekinah is the invisible force of Natural Change.

Autumn

Shekinah animates all Earthly action, moving all things toward wholeness and harmony. Her only interest is integration, bringing together what needs to be united for the good of all. She is Holy Communion and She is Re-Union. For Shekinah also knows what must come apart. She is the ultimate shapeshifter in the realm of the Goddess.

Invite Shekinah into the space around you. You needn't give instruction or direction. She will instinctively begin Her subtle play. Listen to the pulse of Her invisible breath. When you follow fancy and whimsy without reason, you are in Shekinah's magical presence. When you surrender without condition to Her mysterious maneuvers, She will bring you to what is true and real.

The Goddess Book

AFFIRMATION

I can make changes without having rational reasons.
I can trust the unknown without having to fix an outcome.
I pay attention to what is calling me
from deep within my knowing.
I trust the adventure of life.

SELKET

Scorpion Goddess of Magic

S ELKET, the Egyptian Scorpion Goddess of Magic,
guards the gateways of death and rebirth, initiating the
deceased into the Underworld and teaching them the Ways
of radical transformation. In Egypt, Scorpio is the sign of
the Autumn Equinox. As we enter the season of darkness
and unknowing, Selket teaches us how to "die" again and
again and keep on living.

◆ ·1⅟1· ◆

Autumn

Selket is particularly helpful if you're feeling trapped and fragmented by a soul-stifling job. Selket wants to know if you find yourself trying to live the authentic "rest of your life" on the weekends. Listen to the words of the scorpion: This is not your path. This is not the Way.

The passage through Selket's gate is not an intellectual journey. Information never equals transformation. Dying to old ways of thinking, being, and believing comes from the gut.

This week, ask the sphinx-like Selket how you can make your transitions easier. As you bring your awareness into the center of your being, ask Her what needs to "die" in order to truly open to living a joyful path. Be prepared to accept whatever She offers. She may be alarmingly honest. It may feel like a "sting." Within the scorpion's venom is the antidote. The seeds of Spring are always contained in Autumn's harvest.

AFFIRMATION

Change is Natural.
I let go of poisonous, stagnant thinking.
I give thanks for my many blessings.
I let new awarenesses unfold
from the center of my being.

MOMOY

Medicine Woman

THE WORD "medicine" has its origins in ancient Goddess cultures. The Babylonian word for Mother Wisdom was *me*. *Me* also means the magical power of Fate, the sacred presence of the Goddess, healing magic, or medicine. Women were the first midwives and shamans, welcoming the newly arrived and preparing sacred rituals for the departed. The Medicine Woman holds the Moon in Her hands; She trusts divine timing. She knows that all things that once were will be again.

Autumn

Women are encouraged to deny the waxing and waning of our being. We are conditioned to strive for exactitude and perfection. However, reason-driven answers are not the gutsy ways of the Wise Medicine Woman. Her omens are cloaked in mystery. Answers arrived at by reason alone change nothing.

Give yourself a day of sacred medicine, especially if you are feeling "caught up" in someone else's drama. Conserve your time and energy. Put your needs first. It is dangerous to ignore your natural requirements for time "away," just as it is unwise to remain hidden when being called to howl. Periodic returns to the fertile darkness act as preventive medicine. Connecting with dreams, fantasies, forgotten feelings, and distress signals can provide you with the healing insights you may be needing at this time. Like the Moon, you will emerge from your retreat fully refreshed.

AFFIRMATION

I take the time I need
to listen to the whirrings of my soul.
I pay attention to my biological signals,
staying present with discomfort
long enough to hear its healing medicine.
I then change behavior patterns,
creating harmony from the inside out.

INANNA

Queen of Heaven

THE STORY of the Sumerian Goddess Inanna is the initiation of all women. Every step of the way She confronted the ultimate death of an old way of being. She eventually emerged, possessed of Her own power, Her own authority.

Acting as the agent of Her own healing journey, She ventured into the Underworld to meet Her long-forgotten sister, Ereshkigal. Her sister is a symbol of all of Inanna's hopes, dreams, and aspirations that have been ignored, forgotten or denied. Meeting Ereshkigal awakens Inanna's memory.

In order to reclaim the forgotten fragments of Her being, Inanna is required to grieve, mourn, and let die old habits and behaviors that kept Her from true Self-expression.

Autumn

As the light of Summer retreats into Autumn, Inanna invites you into Her kitchen of revisions and crone wisdoms to jog your memory and get to the core of lingering disease, depression, and unhappiness. Is something eating at you? Have you buried your dreams in pursuit of someone else's? Are you holding hostage your dreams and little girl yearnings deep in your belly? Inanna's journey is prompted when She hears something from the "Great Below"; the abyss into which Inanna descends is the interior tomb of the Unknown Self. To deny or ignore what we hold within the recesses of our sacred Woman-spaces is dangerous.

What is your "Great Below," your "depression," saying to you? Listen to the wise voice of your sister within. Challenge old beliefs and fears that may be impeding your steps. It may be time to sort the seeds, stir the soup, and cut the ropes.

AFFIRMATION

I live my life attuned to my True Nature.
I take all the time I need to take care of me.
I make friends with my desires.
I live fully awakened to my Goddess Being.

DEMETER

Goddess of the Harvest

HER NAME MEANS Mother Vulva–the gateway where all things are born and reborn. She was honored with festivals during the seasonal changes of Autumn and Spring, times that signaled the birth and death of the grain. Her mysteries at Eleusis were celebrated for almost two thousand years! The longest running "thanksgiving" ever.

The Romans called Her Ceres, and from Her Roman name we get the word cereal. A most nourishing way to start the day.

♦ 453 ♦

Autumn

In Autumn and Winter, Demeter mourns the loss of Her daughter, Persephone, often called Kore, meaning seed or sprout. While she grieves, the Earth is barren. When Persephone returns as the new green shoots of Spring, Demeter rejoices. Grain and the human life are continuously reborn through the gateway of the Earth, perpetually joined at the root. The myth of Demeter and Persephone/Kore–that of fullness, loss, and return–is also a lunar myth and that of the Triple Goddess–Maiden, Mother, Crone–the most powerful rites of passage in a woman's life.

However far we have strayed from the Eleusinian Mysteries, we are still completely dependent on the Earth for our sustenance. Invite Demeter to feast with you as Autumn's light grows thin. Give thanks for Her many gracious blessings as you pass through the grocery store gates. She lives!

AFFIRMATION

The food I eat is a gift of the Goddess.
Everything I eat nourishes and heals me.
The healthy food I eat becomes a healthy me.

KAMRUSEPAS

Healer Goddess of the Hittites

IN MANY ancient cultures, hair represents powerful life-force energy. Kamrusepas's hair represents energy and powerful female life-force, and here she is combing out Her braid to prepare to work Her healing magic. Through this metaphor of unbraiding, She tells us dis-ease, stagnation, and paralysis can be healed. We can untangle a situation and let go of what needs to go by working with the ideas of relaxation and release. Kamrusepas reminds us that healing flows best when we are open to the energy of the Universe.

Autumn

Kamrusepas addresses root causes, not merely symptoms. As you search for the sacred in the midst of confusion, illness, and catastrophe, call on this ancient Goddess for guidance. Invoking her wisdom requires a conscious commitment to healthy change in all areas of your life.

Sometimes illness is the only way women can care for themselves. Pain is often a distress signal that your life is out of balance. If your body is telling you to change your life, vitamins and exercise alone may not suffice. Core issues involving learned belief systems and self-esteem need re-evaluation. Family issues and work routines must be examined in order to create deep healing.

Lasting, healthy change requires a new way of dancing with the Goddess within. When we tune in to the processes of our own woman bodies, authentic visions of wholeness and healing emerge.

AFFIRMATION

I no longer justify self-care through illness.
I commit my whole being to well-being.
I take care of me, and everything else
falls into perfect harmony.

BAST

Egyptian Cat Goddess of the Moon

Lovely Luna
Feline Queen
How Your Mystery
Dazzles My Skin
Your Smile Is As Subtle
As The Horned Moon Light
Woman Eyed Spirit
Sweet Prancing Heart
I Dance Inside Your Serpent Tale

Autumn

B ast or Bastet, the ancestral Mother of all cats, is the Goddess of joy, dancing, music, and play. She holds a sistrum or rattle in Her right hand and a cat aegis or protective totem in Her left. She is closely associated with Diana, Goddess of the Moon.

Let Bast, the Goddess of Pleasure, lead your way. If you are caught in the patriarchal "no pain, no gain" formula, it's time to give it up. The root word of pleasure is *please*. When we focus on what truly pleases us, we are following a recipe for wholeness of body, mind, and spirit.

Bastet invites us in for snuggling comfort in the Lap of Joy. The simplest things, usually within reach, are the most refreshing. Play old music and dance with a broom. Reread a favorite book. Welcome this eternal and refreshing moment. Imagine being Her kitten. Let this delightful Mother Cat lick you alive and well. "All acts of love and pleasure are my rituals."

AFFIRMATION

I am playful.
I dance in the love light of a benevolent Mother Goddess.
I enjoy the simple things in life.
I enjoy the journey!

UNGNYEO

Power of the Bear

F EMALE healers were the first shamans. The earliest
healing arts included ritual, art-making, plant wisdom,
and ceremony. Shamans ventured into the realm of the
Great Mother, invoking the Mother of All Things, the Dark
Mother, Grandmother Growth, or the Death Goddess for
guidance.

The shamanic trance can be invoked by drumming, dancing, fever, menstruation, childbirth, chanting, yoga, intense
creativity, anger, and near-death experiences; all of which
facilitate the merging of one's personal identity with the
landscape, animals, deities, or ancestors.

◆ 465 ◆

Autumn

Female sexuality, in which intense orgasm can evoke an ecstatic trance, figures prominently in ancient shamanic healing rites. The first religion may have been originated by women and based on sexual-spiritual union: a celebration of body-based cosmic ecstasy and wisdom.

Begin your ecstatic return to wholeness and healing now. Shamanic experiences are not always fun. Although you may feel like you're falling apart, only the shell of your daily identity is cracking in order to release your authentic Self. Ground your energy in healthy ways during these times of spiritual emergence. Imagine an animal ally or the Korean Bear Goddess Ungnyeo guiding your journey. Dance the wisdom of your spirit ally. Let your heightened sexual pleasure reveal a healing vision. Drum the Mother's Wisdom back into your heart.

AFFIRMATION

I am One with the powers of Creation
that reside within.
I take full responsibility for healing me.
Loving myself is a miracle cure.

Autumn

YHI

Goddess of Light and Creation

IN THE LAND of the Dreamtime, Yhi is said to have created all the plants and animals of Australia, as well as the first humans. Creatrix and Sun Goddess, She is shown here with blond hair like the light of the sun rising over the red earth of the Outback, Her body is painted with white streaks like sunrays. In the beginning, women alone knew the secrets of creating the World from their bodies.

Autumn

Centered in the heart, a Goddess way of being opens us to our intuitive knowing and creative potential, honoring our sacred woman bodies as temples of divine inspiration and ecstatic pleasure. Goddess consciousness fosters a return to nature and Earth-honoring principles, restoring and balancing what has so long been lost.

Yhi urges you to stretch your imagination far and wide to include all possibilities. In the moments between reason and justification lie the wild seeds of hope and true harmony. Spontaneous and playful moments hold important messages. Find a meaningful "power" object and carry it with you all day. At bedtime, place it on your nightstand and ask a question about something that has been bothering you. Keep a notepad by your bed for messages that may wake you suddenly. You may want to take a new magical or spiritual name to honor your Goddess Essence.

AFFIRMATION

Every part of me is sacred.
I treasure my creative impulses.
I am a Goddess divine.
I can dream up a new vision for my life plan
and change it any time.
I am my own temple of inspiration.

Autumn

BABA YAGA

Witch of the Forest

IN BALTIC myth, Baba, the old woman of Autumn,
Mother Time, lived in the last kernel of harvested grain,
as the season moved to winter. The woman to eat the Baba
was said to give birth in the Spring. This wise old Baba,
death becoming life, moved into Russian folklore as an Old
Hag of the forest.

Autumn

Before leaving the "season of the witch," the season of the Baba, take time to reclaim Her life-loving wisdom.

A witch is wise to her own power, profoundly connected to self, others, and to Earth. Passion, lust for living, and laughter are her potions.

A witch tells her true feelings. Her passionate, life-loving practices ward off patriarchal oppression. Often "out of line," she enjoys gathering in circles and spiral dances with other witchy women.

A witch is a magician and healer, savvy and self-directed. She resists anything that takes her away from the fullness of living. A witch's reverence for life, beginning with her own, is her antidote for addictions. She knows and cares about herself as much as others, not less than. A witch lives on the Lunatic Fringe, loving her life in tune with the Moon.

AFFIRMATION

I am a witch.
I have the power to change the things that
I do not like in my life.
I find out what I want and need
and I give it to myself.
I no longer hide my beliefs and talents to protect others.
I speak up.
I enjoy every witch way I am.

Winter

SEEDS

Time to whisper

And to listen

Time to soak

Your heart's intentions

Bellow deep the dark's delight

Buzzing soft your own invention

IN THE QUIET stir of Winter, the Sun's light grows stronger each day. Renew your awareness of the Goddess and find the source and strength of your inner creative magic with the help of Spider Woman and the following meditation.

Light a white candle. Invoke Spider Woman into the room by calling Her name aloud three times. Sit comfortably. Place both hands on your lower abdomen, over your womb. Take long, slow, even breaths without forcing your breathing pattern. Relax into your breath. Relax into your body.

Imagine a doorway at the top of your head. Imagine that your breath enters your body through the top of your head and exits through your womb, passing through your hands that are now resting on your belly. As your breath passes through the door at your crown and out your womb,

The Goddess Book

you imagine a silver-white, wispy thread linking you with Spider Woman and the vast reservoir of energy that brings all things into being. Let your thread of connectedness get stronger, like a rope or a braided vine. Feel your energy joining with Spider Woman's energy, pulsing and vibrating along your woven cord. Relaxing deeply, you feel a gentle tug on the rope as you are led along a forest path into a dreamy Winter scene. Spider Woman has woven three messages for you into the landscape of dancing light.

When you're ready, open your eyes. In your journal, draw the doorway at the top of your head and the thread of connectedness streaming from your womb. What messages are revealed in Spider Woman's Winter landscape?

SHEELA NA GIG

Guardian of Good Fortune

THIS NAKED and squatting Goddess from pagan Ireland is the guardian of good fortune. Ancient worshippers would touch Her in passing for good luck. Her bold and bawdy gesture and enigmatic expression suggest She has an "in" on the secrets of life and surely knows which road to take to get there.

The Sheela Na Gig may have served the same purpose in Irish myth as the Baubo in ancient Greece: a ribald, Crone clown. The well-being of the world depends on relieving female sadness, restoring joy, love, laughter, and sensual pleasure.

◆ 184 ◆

Winter

Imagine passing through Her gate of plenty, returning her impish grin. What does it feel like to observe such an unblushingly presumptuous image of woman-ness? Is there anything that makes you uncomfortable? If so, where does your discomfort come from; who taught you about your body?

Welcome the Sheela into your life. She reminds you that no matter where you are, you've always got your act together. You never need push yourself to prove yourself. Partake of Her playful capers. Adorn yourself in gaudy baubles. Dance Her erotic jig, letting your hips wiggle and wobble. Sing praises to your own silky rich vulva cave. Massage your yoni with sweet fragrant oil. End your ritual expression with a blessing for the healing of all womankind.

AFFIRMATION

I enjoy the sensual pleasures of my woman body.
I am reclaiming and reinventing my life.
I can be spontaneously quirky and curious,
exploring the many expressions of my woman-being.

SOPHIA

Holy Wisdom

HOLY SOPHIA–Holy Wisdom–was once revered as the primal Earth Goddess, the original Craftmaker of Life. According to a Gnostic creation myth, the primordial female power, Silence, gave birth to Wisdom. And the World Soul was born from Wisdom's smile. Interesting that a woman's cervix becomes a crescent "smile" after giving birth.

Today, in the growing light of Winter, Sophia returns. She is the ever-moving, sacred center around which the spiral of life spins.

Winter

S ilent, but not forgotten, Wisdom lies hidden, residing
in all things. Sophia waits in our personal experiences:
playful and painful, poignant and joyful. And She waits in
our dreams. She sits at the door, calling Her children into
Her temple of serendipitous strolls, poetic visions, creative
musings, spontaneous laughter, and the fiery pleasures of
love. In metaphor and metaform, She mediates from our
Woman Souls.

Yes, the Goddess of Wisdom is the ultimate Arouser.
To those who return Her love with heartfelt reverence,
the hearth is kept warm. Listen to Her voice, the one that
whispers from within. What was relevant yesterday may not
suffice today. Paradoxically, the past will reveal the precise
information you are seeking. Sophianic solutions will arise.
Nothing can delay Wisdom's return. Once invoked, She
will lead you to your true destiny.

AFFIRMATION

Inner wisdom is my road map.
I can say, "I don't know," when I don't know.
When I do know,
I can speak until I'm clearly understood.

SPIDER WOMAN

The Source

A T THE DAWN of Being, Spider Woman spun the
first silver threads from Her own body. When She
finished weaving the four directions, She sat at the center of
the Universe, singing in a tender, deep voice. As She sang,
She gave birth to two daughters who helped her create the
Sun, Moon, Earth, and Star People. From the red clay of
Earth, She created all people. From Her Spider being, She
connected a web to each being, keeping a doorway at the
top of each person's head open. By chanting Spider Woman's song of creation each person keeps the doorway open,
always connected to Her creative wisdom–always connected
to each other.

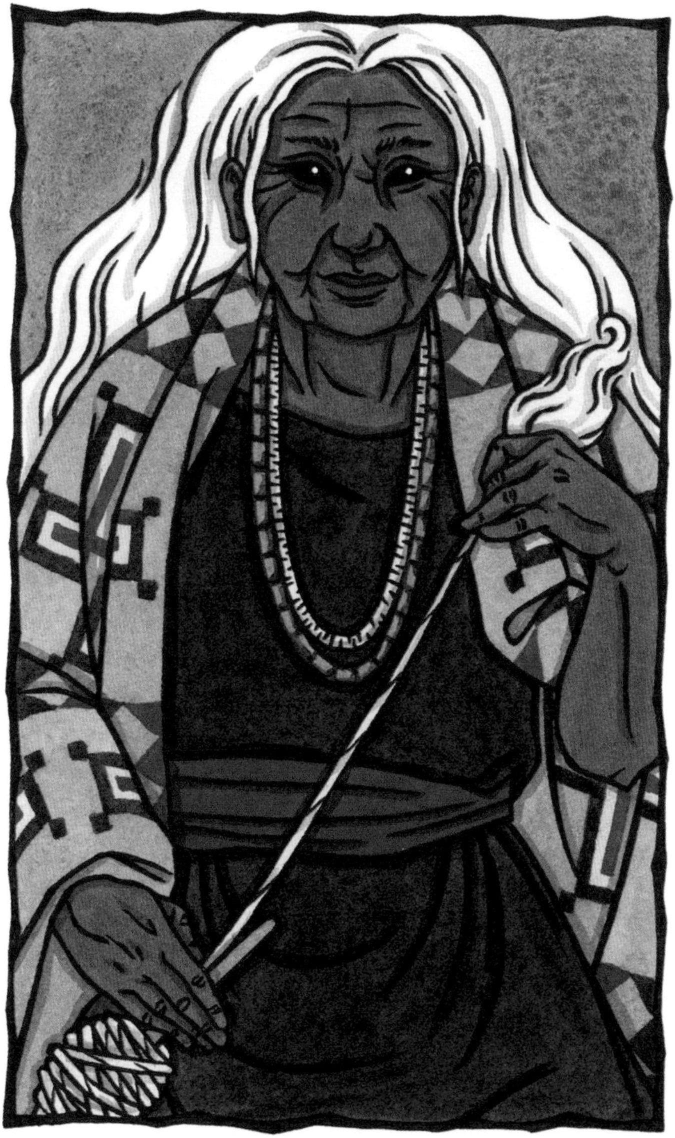

Winter

Spider Woman is calling you home. This Winter week, take time to remember Her song. Let Her remind you of your own creative magic. Keep the doorways open to the cosmic creative flow that inspired the beginnings of all life.

By remaining connected to your own creative spirit, you stay in touch with the sacred power of Spider Woman, weaving together the magic of the Universe and your own unique vision. Love your ideas into being. Love what you create. Love what you make of your life.

AFFIRMATION

I have fun creating.
I am uniquely creative in thought,
word, and action.
I follow the pathway
of my creative inspiration.

KALI

Goddess of Destruction and Creation

IN INDIA, Kali Mahadevi is the powerful Triune Goddess of creation, preservation, and radical transformation. She is raw female instinct, always changing, always changeless. She opens Herself up and gives birth to Ultimate Reality. She closes Herself and gathers everything into the latent darkness, the seed-state. In endless and alternating patterns of opening and closing, Kali brings into existence countless Universes. She is Shakti, Female Force, "Cosmic Energy." Wise ones say that to treat a woman, a Shakti, badly is a crime. For without Shakti, there is stagnation.

Kali hurls Herself into action, leaping with creative potential, transforming Her world.

Winter

A Kali woman knows when to snap Herself out of Self-destructive patterns and power trips. She moves from Her guts, and she has the power to make changes because she can name what is disturbing Her. Kali speaks Her woman mind. She thumbs Her nose, sticks out Her tongue, and kicks up Her heels in outrageous acts of passion. Kali activates change by cutting through illusions and distractions.

Kali encourages you to trust your discomfort as a signal for change. Seek out loving and supportive friends at this time. Let go of stale relationships that do not support you at your Shakti best. Practice standing before the mirror and sticking out your tongue in a gesture of Kali solidarity. Courage, compassion, and daring are yours when you need them this week. Be willing to accept and value the whole of your being even when others may not.

Remember: When women smile, we bare our teeth.

AFFIRMATION

I am whole, holy, and free.
I know best what is best for me.
This is my life,
and I am creating it the way I want it.
I make up my own mind.
And I can change my mind anytime.

LILITH

Night Creature

ACCORDING to Hebrew tradition, Lilith was Adam's first wife. He tried to force Her into the patriarchal missionary position of lovemaking. Unwilling to submit, She returned to Her people of the Red Sea to live a life of Her own, practicing sacred sex in communion with the Goddess. A more subdued Eve was put into position, and Lilith was bad-mouthed as a demon renegade.

Winter

The new millennium belongs to Lilith. It's time to sing holy praises to those Wild Cats, Witches, and Night Hags who refuse to participate in systems of dominance and oppression. Time to invite Lilith back into our lovemaking body-minds of sensual pleasure .

During the next few days, practice living a radically sensual, Lilith-inspired life. Perform acts of Self-Loving: they are strong political statements. Defy the death-dealing media and turn off your television. Let each moment be a spontaneous response to the beauty of the natural world.

As the Winter sun warms the Earth, let the subtle Winter light stir your body and soul. Make love in the glow of the Goddess. Hear yourself humming, moaning, and hissing with ecstasy.

Smile, laugh, giggle, snort, chortle, and love more.

Lilith is back home to stay.

AFFIRMATION

I refuse to let the opinions of others
determine my state of mind.
I am in charge of my thoughts and feelings.
I stop worrying.
I choose happiness first.
I open to the pleasures of my life.

AIDA WEDO

Rainbow Serpent

FROM BENEATH the World came Rainbow Serpent, stretching into the sky. There She gave birth to the First People of Australia. To this day the Australian Aborigines are in contact with the living myth of the Rainbow Serpent through the "dreamtime," a contiguous reality rich with sacred-source visions.

Knowing the dynamics of your own personal mythology is crucial to healing yourself. What you inherit, consciously or unconsciously, from the woman who gave birth to you makes a big impact on how you live your life. The past works through you every day, like a "dreamtime" occurring not as a separate reality, but here and now.

Winter

Exploring your family story is a good place to begin personal healing, particularly if you experience recurring health problems. Our bodies know the truth. An internal struggle, disease, occurs when that knowledge is consciously contradicted. Often, uncovering one small "secret" can confirm what your body has known all along. It's the great big Aha!

During the days of Winter, make an effort to find out more about your personal myth. Let the Rainbow Mother take you where you need to go. Who are the women in your matriarchal line? Most women can name women only one generation back. The information you uncover may initiate a grieving process. Remember the word "mourn" means "remember."

AFFIRMATION

I open to my complete healing.
I am given the information I need to know.
I release to the Universe
what does not belong to me.

BRIGIT

Lady of the Flame

FEBRUARY 1st is the feast day of Brigit or Bright One,
Lady of the Flame, Celtic Triple Mother, Queen of
the Land. She is the Celtic Goddess of poetry, medicine,
inspiration, and smithcraft. Brigit invented whistling as a
secret signal to call Her friends in time of need. She is often
seen carrying a cauldron, representing Her Divine powers of
creation and transformation.

Winter

When invoking Brigit, first light a candle. Then place a chair opposite yours to welcome Her into the room. Take a deep breath and let the air escape slowly between your teeth, whistling as you exhale. Imagine the presence of an awesome Queen filling the room. You feel Her intense warmth as a tingling sensation in your hands and feet.

Share your most pressing concerns with Her by asking three questions. Her feast day is also called Imbolc, meaning "in the belly." Let your questions emanate from the deepest part of your Being. Throughout the week, Brigit will guide you. Notice any unexpected or coincidental events. Go with your hunches. If you lose your way, just give a whistle and wait for Brigit's fiery warmth to bring you back to your center. In the dark of winter, the seeds of spring are vibrating with quiet expectancy,

AFFIRMATION

I use my imagination to brightly enrich my life.
I no longer need to rush around trying to make things happen.
Bright blessings easily flow into my life.
I make room for unexpected, joyful surprises.

GORGON

Cunning One

THE GREEKS called the Crone Goddess of the Libyan Amazons, Medusa, the Cunning One. With Her two sisters Stheno, Strength, and Euryale, Wide Roaming One, they represent the serpent-haired priestesses of the Triple Moon Goddess. They wore red-painted masks, gorgoneions, representing a woman's healing "wise blood" and the Moon's regenerative power.

The Gorgon wants to know how you dance with anger. She encourages you to unmask your feelings.

Winter

Anger repressed for too long often shows up as compulsions, addictions, or chronic hostility. Fits of sobbing and choking tears are often anger's disguise. Denying feelings blocks the healing "red" power of the Gorgon.

Take time this week to write in your journal about who or what is the source of disharmony in your everyday life. Include minor irritations. Over time, considerable tension can accumulate from petty disturbances. Pay attention to your feelings as you write. Imagine your Gorgon sisters, Strength and Wide Roaming One, helping you gain insight.

The Gorgon's most powerful magic is effective communication. Telling your truth, including asking others to take responsibility for their behavior, may take you beyond the veneer of comfort created by a smiling mask of compliance. Once you have shown your true face, you are ready to don the wise guise of the Gorgon.

AFFIRMATION

I own all my feelings and I set them free.
I can feel angry and simply say so.
I release my deepest wounds in safe, supportive ways.
I dance to the tune of the Moon
in ecstasy and bliss.

FREYA

Lady of Love

THE GODDESS Freya brought light to the peoples of northern Europe. She gave them the heat of the forge and the fire of sexual love. She also taught divination to the holy Volva, female prophets who did ecstatic dances and offered glimpses into the future. Although, like Kali, she was a Triple Goddess, Her essence was sexual love.

Winter

Imagine standing on a hill in the clear wind and sunlight of Winter. The trees of a sacred grove surround you. The rich smell of the evergreen pine relaxes you. You feel "at home," grounded in pulsing Earth energies that stream up your legs, through your spine, and back down again. You invoke Freya by calling out Her name. She appears before you wearing a magic amber necklace and a golden, shimmering cloak. You ask Her guidance about a love relationship. She smiles and whispers an auspicious word or two in your ear.

When you open your eyes, write your vision of Freya in your journal. Include as many details as possible. Make a "love charm" from cloth, buttons, yarn, thread–anything you have around the house that seems appropriate. Include a small clipping of hair. Pubic hair is very powerful in love charms! Sing your heartfelt desires as you cast your love spell. Keep your charm on your altar on Fridays, Freya's sacred day. See what the Goddess brings.

AFFIRMATION

The Goddess Freya guides my loving way.
Expressing myself intimately and sexually
brings me joy.
Loving is easy.

DREAMING PRIESTESS

Inspiration and Creation

THE DREAMING Priestess represents a trance-channeling goddess. In temples around the world, seers practiced the healing arts, and in these temples pilgrims could spiral into a sacred space, finding wisdom and healing within.

Enter the temple of your Dreams as the Sun's rays lengthen and illuminate the remaining days of Winter. Much of what you meet here is eager to be found.

Winter

Your dreams may not always provide direct solutions, but playing in the realm of dreams opens you to sacred wisdom. When you least expect it, the meaning will be revealed, offering you a surprising gift.

As you lie in bed, imagine that you are walking through the underground maze of a Goddess temple. You feel your way along the smooth wall, moving always inward. Eventually you enter the room at the heart of the labyrinth. A priestess awaits you. You tell her what troubles you most. She motions to you to lie on the soft bed beside her. Breathing deeply, you drift into a soothing sleep. When you awake, write and draw the images, messages, or felt senses of your dreams in a journal. Avoid analyzing the outcome or straining for "results." Winter opens into Spring without effort. Let your magic unfold in the same way.

AFFIRMATION

I remember my dreams.
I am an open channel for the voice of the Goddess,
whatever she may say.
I am willing to listen and act upon
the inspiration of my dreams.

NU KUA

Creatrix Goddess

IN ANCIENT Chinese myth, Nu Kua is the divine fore-mother of humanity. She is one of the oldest and most powerful of the female deities from one of Earth's oldest civilizations. Some legends separate her into a male named Nu and a female named Kua, and these were the first humans. She is the creator of life from the primordial chaos of the Universe and put the land, sea, and sky into their proper places. She brought civilization to Earth. She is often called She Who Is All, yin and yang.

The eighth day of the Chinese new year celebrates the birthday of humanity, which was fashioned by Nu Kua.

Winter

Nu Kua represents the opportunity for restoration and order after chaos. She is the tempering influence that calms situations and brings levelheadedness. She represents a return to innocence and the ability to adopt new positive attitudes.

If the fog of Winter has you questioning your direction, pursuits, and purpose, invoke the Goddess Nu Kua. She reminds you to focus your attention on the priorities of the moment. The art of paying deep attention is a sacred faculty.

The journey from Winter to Spring is often difficult. For those with patience and power, miracles unfold. Beware of those people and things that may distract you from your true course. Nu Kua reminds you that calm will always be restored in stressful times, and She helps you retain an attitude of strength after difficult events might leave you feeling jaded.

AFFIRMATION

I live in the moment of all possibilities.
I can handle whatever comes my way.
I use Wise Woman power tools to keep me in touch
with my Divine Direction.
I love and accept myself
no matter where I am on my path
of Self-uncovery.

HEKATE

Guardian of the Crossroads

QUEEN of the Witches, Hekate is the Holy Crone. In Greece, Hekate was honored as the Guardian of the Crossroads. Wherever three roads met, the *trivia*, there She waited. To those who honored Her, understanding the inevitabilities of life, She bestowed Her wisdom.

In the Trinity of the Great Goddess, Hekate represents the menopausal woman, she who no longer bleeds in rhythm with the Moon. In the Goddess tradition, this is a powerful rite of passage. Her wisdom informed by time, a Hekate Woman now joins the council of Elders with dignity and grace.

Winter

When standing at the Crossroads of Change, or whenever you need a Grand Mother's guidance, invoke Hekate. She teaches us how to make friends with ambiguity, chaos, endings, death, mixed-up feelings, the unknown, and the scary by accepting what cannot be controlled. Mostly, Hecate asks all women to befriend our beloved bodies, particularly during times of enormous biorhythmic changes.

In the midst of any transition, take time to nurture yourself. Our bodies are not separate from what goes on around them. Eat healthy foods, take long walks, talk with trees, light candles, say prayers, and consult with other women who may have faced or are facing similar situations. Call together a circle of howling Hecate Women to share stories and experiences. However, don't be surprised if what you need comes from the voice of a child. The unexpected and the "trivial" hold extraordinary clues.

AFFIRMATION

I accept this moment as it is.
I enjoy the freedom of letting go
of the need to control the results.
I can dawdle, drift, dally, linger, and wander.
I make my own rules to live by.

PYTHIA

The Wisdom Oracle

MOST REVERED in early Goddess cultures is none other than the Wise Crone, Seer, and Soothsayer, for only a woman past 50 years of age could be called by the name "oracle." Only a woman past her childbearing years, with an embodied accumulation of wisdom and knowledge, was allowed to channel and endure the truth spoken through the sacred Earth shrine at Delphi, which means womb. On the seventh day of each lunar month, Pythia sat on her tripod throne, chewing bay leaves. In an altered state of consciousness, Her oracular visions were often vaguely understandable, always enigmatic and shrouded in the sublime.

Winter

Imagine that you arrive at the Oracle of Delphi. The Prophetess Pythia sits before you. She is smiling wryly. Her eyes are focused and wide open, staring straight into yours. She is always moving, wiggling, shifting. You smell the strong sweet fragrance of bay as a white steamy mist spirals up around her. She is holding a writhing colorful snake, round, fat, and friendly. The tiny snake tongue that whips in and out mesmerizes you. You feel oddly relaxed and trusting. You sense a strong reverence for this Wise Familiar One.

Where have you seen her before? In the grocery store aisles? In a yoga class? In those photos of aunts and cousins from family albums? Yes, Pythia is your kin. What one question do you ask Pythia today?

AFFIRMATION

The wisdom of all my ancestors pulses in my body.
I honor my spiritual guides.
I am an open channel for compassion and understanding.
I receive new information for a life
of inner peace and joy.
I believe in me.

Sources

Achterberg, Jeanne. *Woman as Healer*. Boston: Shambhala, 1991.

Ardinger, Barbara. *A Woman's Book of Rituals & Celebrations*. San Rafael, CA: New World Library, 1995.

Austen, Hallie Iglehart. *The Heart of the Goddess: Art, Myth, and Meditations of the World's Sacred Feminine*. Oakland, CA: Wingbow Press, 1990.

Baring, Anne, and Jules Cashford. *The Myth of the Goddess: Evolution of an Image*. New York: Viking Arkana, 1991.

Borton, Joan C. *Drawing from the Women's Well: Reflections on the Life Passage of Menopause*. CA: LuraMedia, 1992.

Blair, Nancy. *Amulets of the Goddess: Oracles of Ancient Wisdom*. Oakland, CA: Wingbow Press, 1993.

———. *Clay: The Earth Mother Way. Creativity and Healing Workshops for Women*. Unpublished notes. 1994-1995.

Cartwright, Kate, and Alexandra Hart. *Goddesses: Images for Coloring & Meditation*. CA: Concepts Publishing, 1994.

Chernin, Kim. *The Hungry Self: Women, Eating, and Identity*. New York: Harper & Row, 1985.

———. *The Obsession: Reflections on the Tyranny of Slenderness*. New York: Harper Colophon Books, 1981.

———. *Reinventing Eve: Modern Woman in Search of Herself*. New York: Times Books, 1987.

Conway, D. J. *Maiden, Mother, Crone: The Myth and Reality of the Triple Goddess*. St. Paul, MN: Llewellyn Publications, 1994.

Demetrakopoulos, Stephanie. *Listening to Our Bodies: The Rebirth of Feminine Wisdom*. Boston: Beacon Press, 1983.

Diaz, Adriana. *Freeing the Creative Spirit*. New York: HarperCollins, 1992.

Edwards, Carolyn McVickar. *The Storyteller's Goddess*. New York: HarperCollins, 1991.

Ellis, Normandi. *Dreams of Isis: A Woman's Spiritual Sojourn*. Wheaton, IL: Quest Books, 1994.

Estes, Clarissa Pinkola. *Women Who Run with the Wolves*. New York: Ballantine Books, 1992.

Francia, Luisa. *Dragontime: Magic and Mystery of Menstruation*. Woodstock, NY: Ash Tree 1988.

Frazer, Sir James George. *The Golden Bough: A Study in Magic and Religion*. New York: MacMillan, 1951.

Gadon, Elinor W. *The Once and Future Goddess*. New York: Harper & Row Publishers, 1989.

George, Demetra. *Mysteries of the Dark Moon: The Healing Power of the Dark Goddess*. San Francisco: HarperCollins, 1992.

Getty, Adele. *Goddess: Mother of Living Nature*. New York: Thames and Hudson, 1990.

Gimbutas, Marija. *The Language of the Goddess*. San Francisco: Harper & Row, 1989.

———. *The Civilization of the Goddess*. San Francisco: HarperSanFrancisco, 1991.

Grahn, Judy. *Blood, Bread, and Roses: How Menstruation Created the World*. Boston: Beacon Press, 1993.

Harris, Maria. *Dance of the Spirit*. New York: Bantam Books, 1989.

Hay, Louise L. *You Can Heal Your Life*. Carlsbad, CA: Hay House, 1984.

Hutchinson, Marcia Germaine. *Transforming Body Image: Learning to Love the Body You Have*. Trumansburg, NY: The Crossing Press, 1985.

Johnson, Buffie. *Lady of the Beasts: Ancient Images of the Goddess and Her Sacred Animals.* San Francisco: HarperCollins, 1988.

Lubell, Winifred Milius. *The Metamorphosis of Baubo: Myths of Woman's Sexual Energy.* Nashville, TN: Vanderbilt University Press, 1994.

Matthews, Caitlin. *Sophia: Goddess of Wisdom. The Divine Feminine from Black Goddess to World Soul.* London: Mandala, 1991.

McLuhan, T. C. *The Way of the Earth.* New York: Simon & Schuster, 1994.

Monaghan, Patricia. *The Book of Goddesses and Heroines.* St. Paul, MN: Llewellyn Publications, 1990.

——. *O Mother Sun!* Freedom, CA: Crossing Press, 1994.

Mookerjee, Ajit. *Kali: The Feminine Force.* Rochester, VT: Destiny Books, 1988.

Nicholson, Shirley, comp. *The Goddess Re-Awakening: The Feminine Principle Today.* London, England: The Theosophical Publishing House, 1989.

——, and Brenda Rosen, comp. *Gaia's Hidden Life: The Unseen Intelligence of Nature.* Wheaton, IL: Quest Books, 1992.

Noble, Vicki. *Motherpeace: A Way to the Goddess through Myth, Art, and Tarot.* San Francisco: HarperCollins, 1983.

——. *Shakti Woman: Feeling Our Fire, Healing Our World–The New Female Shamanism.* San Francisco: HarperCollins, 1991.

——, ed. *Uncoiling the Snake.* San Francisco: HarperCollins, 1993.

Northrup, Christiane, MD. *Women's Bodies, Women's Wisdom.* New York: Bantam Books, 1994.

Perera, Sylvia Brinton. *Descent to the Goddess: A Way of Initiation for Women.* Toronto: Inner City Books, 1981.

Salmonson, Jessica Amanda. *The Encyclopedia of Amazons.* New York: Doubleday Books, 1991.

Sams, Jamie, and David Carson. *Medicine Cards: The Discovery of Power through the Ways of Animals.* Santa Fe, NM: Bear & Company, 1988.

Schaef, Anne Wilson. *Meditations for Women Who Do Too Much.* San Francisco: HarperCollins, 1990.

Shuttle, Penelope, and Peter Redgrove. *The Wise Wound: The Myths, Realities, and Meanings of Menstruation.* New York: Bantam Books, 1990.

Sjoo, Monica, and Barbara Mor. *The Great Cosmic Mother: Rediscovering the Religion of the Earth.* San Francisco: HarperCollins, 1991.

Starhawk. *Truth or Dare: Encounters with Power, Authority, and Mystery.* New York: Harper & Row, 1987.

Stone, Merlin. *Ancient Mirrors of Womanhood: A Treasury of Goddess and Heroine Lore from Around the World.* Boston: Beacon Press, 1990.

Streep, Peg. *Sanctuaries of the Goddess.* New York: Little, Brown and Co., 1994.

Walker, Barbara G. *The Crone: Woman of Age, Wisdom, and Power.* HarperSanFrancisco, 1985.

——. *The Woman's Encyclopedia of Myths and Secrets.* San Francisco: Harper & Row, 1983.

Weed, Susun S. *Menopausal Years.* Woodstock, NY: Ash Tree Publishing, 1992.

——. *Wise Woman Herbal: Healing Wise.* Woodstock, NY: Ash Tree Publishing, 1989.

Wilshire, Donna. *Virgin, Mother, Crone.* Rochester, VT: Inner Traditions, 1994.

Wolkstein, Diane, and Samuel Noah Kramer. *Inanna: Queen of Heaven and Earth.* New York: Harper & Row Publishers, 1983.

About the Author

NANCY BLAIR is an author, artist, teacher, and environmental activist. She is the author of *The Goddess Book, Goddess Days, Goddesses for Every Season,* and *Amulets of the Goddess: Oracle of Ancient Wisdom,* a guidebook and divination set of twenty-seven discs, intricately carved with images of the Goddess from cultures around the world.

Her memoir, *Thank You, Your Opinion Means Nothing to Me: A Year of Hot Flashes, Flashbacks, and Finding My Voice,* is a hilarious, poignant and wickedly delicious diary that embraces The Change with spiritual insight and wisdom.

Blair earned a Master's Degree of Fine Arts from Rutgers University, Mason Gross School of the Arts. Her artwork has been commissioned by the Museum of Fine Arts, Boston, and Oliver Stone's *The Doors Project,* among others. Her art is in the collection of Sir Elton John as well as many private collections nationally and internationally.

Nancy is currently teaching, writing, and creating art at her home and studio in Florida. For more information about her art or to book an appointment for a reading, visit her on Facebook or at *nancyblair.art.* Follow her on Instagram: *@nancyblair324.*

About the Illustrator

THALIA TOOK is an artist and Pagan with the devoted and passionate goal of painting or writing about every single Goddess ever. Luckily, she also believes in reincarnation because one lifetime will not be long enough to explore the endless beauty, character, and diversity of Woman. But Thalia can think of no better way of spending her life.

Thalia lives in an old New England colonial that is probably haunted, though they're nice enough, for ghosts. Her home has six fireplaces—with a cauldron in each—and six cats, one of whom is the illustrious Aleister Meowley.

Her Goddess art and writings can be found at *thaliatook.com.*